LEARNING ABOUT
PRAYER

Lois Rock

Illustrated by Maureen Galvani

LION
Children's Books

Text by Lois Rock
Illustrations copyright © 2002 Maureen Galvani
This edition copyright © 2002 Lion Publishing

The moral rights of the author and illustrator
have been asserted

Published by
Lion Publishing plc
Mayfield House, 256 Banbury Road
Oxford OX2 7DH, England
www.lion-publishing.co.uk
ISBN 0 7459 4735 2

First edition 2002
1 3 5 7 9 10 8 6 4 2 0

Acknowledgments
The Lord's Prayer on page 3 is taken from Matthew 6:9–13.
The Bible extract on page 9 is taken from Numbers 6:24.
Scriptures quoted from the Good News Bible published by
The Bible Societies/HarperCollins Publishers Ltd, UK
© American Bible Society 1966, 1971, 1976, 1992,
used with permission.

A catalogue record for this book is available
from the British Library

Typeset in 16/26 Carmina Light BT
Printed and bound in Singapore

Introduction: What is prayer?

 Prayer means spending time with God.

When you spend time with a friend, you often talk. You also listen. Sometimes you just sit quietly together.

Christians believe that praying to God is like that… it is like being with a very special kind of friend. This book will tell you more about what Christians mean by prayer.

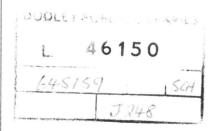

1 Who is a prayer to?

When Christians pray, they pray to their God.

Sometimes they begin as if they were speaking to a grand person: 'O God'.

Sometimes they begin in the same way that people begin a letter: 'Dear God'.

Sometimes they use a title – words that say something about who God is: 'O Lord' or 'Heavenly Father'. There are many more titles.

Sometimes they begin with whatever they really want to say, and they believe that God will hear them.

Christians speak to God in prayer with respect and trust.

2 Do people have to say prayers really loud for God to hear?

Christians believe that God cannot be seen but is everywhere and knows everything.

They believe God can hear a prayer even if they say it by thinking.

Sometimes they say their prayers aloud, but quietly, even if they are alone.

When they meet with other Christians, they often say prayers quite loudly so they can all hear and think the prayer too, if they want.

Christians believe that God hears every kind of prayer, loud or silent.

3 Does a prayer have to have special words?

Christians believe that God understands a person's prayer, no matter which words they choose.

Jesus, the one whom Christians follow, gave his followers a short and simple prayer to use:

'Our Father in heaven:

May your holy name be honoured;

may your Kingdom come;

may your will be done on earth as it is in heaven.

Give us today the food we need.

Forgive us the wrongs we have done,

as we forgive the wrongs that others have done to us.

Do not bring us to hard testing,

but keep us safe from the Evil One.'

Christians pray to God with simple words, such as the ones Jesus taught.

4 Do people have to learn prayers or can they make them up?

Christians believe that prayer is what people say to God from the heart.

Their own prayers are very important to God, even if the words don't seem very clever.

Christians also use prayers that they learn in other ways: prayers that they find in the Bible and prayers written by other Christians.

Sometimes, they ask other Christians to pray for them.

Whatever the words, Christians believe that real prayer is from the heart.

5 Isn't there a magic word that makes a prayer real?

Many Christians end their prayers with a special word: 'Amen'.

It simply means 'let it be so'.

It isn't magic, and it doesn't have to be said at all, but all over the world it is a traditional way of marking the end of a prayer.

When Christians pray together, one person may say the prayers aloud and they will all join in the 'Amen', to show that they are joining in the whole prayer.

 Christians believe that prayer is real because God is listening.

6 Aren't some prayers to Jesus?

Christians believe that Jesus is God's Son.

They believe that Jesus also hears their prayers, and they often pray to Jesus. Sometimes it seems easier to pray to the God-who-is-Jesus because Jesus has been a human being just like everyone. It is easy to picture what he is like and to imagine talking to him.

Their prayers may begin like this: 'Dear Jesus', 'Lord Jesus' or 'Christ Jesus'. 'Christ' is a title, meaning 'God's chosen king'.

Sometimes they pray to God but end their prayers with the words 'in Jesus' name'.

Christians believe that Jesus hears their prayers.

7 Do people have to sit in a special way to pray?

There are several different traditions for how people pray.

Some Christians kneel to pray.

Some stand up.

Some hold their hands up.

Some put their hands together.

Some look up, while others look down, and others close their eyes.

Whatever the tradition they usually follow, they believe that God will always hear them, whenever they pray.

Christians believe that God hears their prayers whatever they are doing.

8 Do people have to go to a special place to pray?

Christians like to meet to learn about God and to worship God. Their gathering is called a church.

They will pray wherever they gather: sometimes in a room in a house, sometimes in a church building.

Jesus told his followers to make their own prayer a quiet and private thing. He said that they could go into a room and close the door.

He himself sometimes went off for a walk to pray on his own in the countryside.

Christians think prayer is not something to show off about – it is between the people praying and God.

 Christians believe that they can pray in any place where, in their heart, they are alone with God.

9 Is there a special time to pray?

Christians believe that God cares for the world day and night. They believe they can pray to God at any time.

Sometimes they set aside a special time to pray, either alone or together.

Some say a prayer as the day begins...

before they eat a meal...

before they begin a journey...

and so on.

One tradition is to say a prayer asking for God's blessing before they go to sleep.

Here is a blessing from the Bible, which is often said as a night-time prayer:

'May the Lord bless you and take care of you.'

Christians believe that God hears their prayers at any time of day or night.

10 If you ask God for things, do you get them?

Christians believe that God wants people to enjoy life and all the good things it can bring.

They also believe that what makes people really happy is to be a close friend to God.

As they pray, God can help them to see what is important to happiness and what is not.

Christians believe that God wants to give people good things.

11 If you pray for something bad, will it happen?

Christians believe that God is all good, and that God will never make anything bad happen.

Sometimes people who pray to God are very angry and they ask for bad things.

Christians believe that God will listen to them with great kindness. They also believe that God will help them find a good way out of being angry, and a good way to deal with the problem.

 Christians believe that prayer can only do good things, because God is good.

12 If God knows everything, why do people need to pray at all?

Christians believe that God already knows what people think and believe and need and want.

They also believe that people were made to be friends with God. Spending time in prayer helps to build that friendship.

As they pray, they begin to see things the way God sees them.

They say that changes everything!

They have begun a great friendship that they believe in their hearts will last for ever and ever.

 Christians believe that prayer helps them to be friends with God for ever.

What is prayer?

1   Christians speak to God in prayer with respect and trust.

2   Christians believe that God hears every kind of prayer, loud or silent.

3   Christians pray to God with simple words, such as the ones Jesus taught.

4   Whatever the words, Christians believe that real prayer is from the heart.

5   Christians believe that prayer is real because God is listening.

6   Christians believe that Jesus hears their prayers.

7   Christians believe that God hears their prayers whatever they are doing.

8   Christians believe that they can pray in any place where, in their heart, they are alone with God.

9   Christians believe that God hears their prayers at any time of day or night.

10 Christians believe that God wants to give people good things.

11 Christians believe that prayer can only do good things, because God is good.

12 Christians believe that prayer helps them to be friends with God for ever.